FOLK COSTUME
OF EASTERN EUROPE

Feast-day dresses from Posavina, Pec district, and Kosovo, Serbia (Yugoslavia)

FOLK COSTUME
OF EASTERN EUROPE

LILLA M. FOX

Illustrated by the author

Headdress from Nizhny Novgorod,
Great Russia

Publishers PLAYS, INC. *Boston*

Library of Congress Cataloging in Publication Data

Fox, Lilla Margaret.
    Folk costume of Eastern Europe.
    SUMMARY: Examines the characteristics of representative costumes from the
various countries and regions of Eastern Europe and how they are influenced
by climate, geography, and historical events.
    1. Costume – Europe, Eastern – Juvenile literature.
[1. Costume – Europe, Eastern]   I. Title.
GT720.F57 1977   391'.00947   76–51358
ISBN 0–8238–0213–2

Printed in Great Britain

Dancers from Byelorussia

Contents

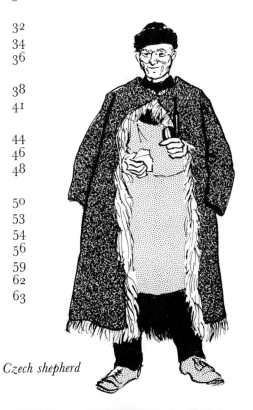

Czech shepherd

Slavic "white costume",
Lublin district, Poland

Albanian city dress
showing Turkish influence

Introduction

There are so many countries in Eastern Europe—the European republics of the Soviet Union together exceed in area all the rest of Europe—and so many regions in each country, and so many different folk costumes in each region, and so many kinds of each costume, whether for dancing, weddings, spring festivities or any other special occasion, that we would need many books to give you an idea of the full richness and variety to be found there. So we have chosen a few, a tiny bunch of flowers from a huge garden, and hope you will find out more for yourself.

On the whole, the costumes of Eastern Europe are older than those of the west, and less influenced by the world of fashion. Conquerors came and went, and national frontiers changed again and again, but the peasants, especially those in mountain regions, lived their own lives, wore their own costumes, and copied from their conquerors only what they wished. Until recently, many never questioned their position: peasants they were and so would dress. They were proud of their traditional ways, and that means a rich heritage of folk arts of all kinds, including costume.

We are used to seeing handsome young folk dancers wearing costumes made from modern materials, and so we can easily forget that many peasants were homely people who became wrinkled and bent with toil, and that their clothes were heavy and bulky. As an example, let us look at three taken from a photograph of about fifty years ago. The peasants illustrated on page 9 come from the mountains of Transylvania where, as in the rest of Europe at one time or another, flax and hemp were grown to make linen and stronger hempen cloth, used for shirts, chemises, aprons and summer skirts and trousers. The flax or hemp had to be sown, harvested, and prepared in various ways, including soaking, beating, drying, and sorting into different weights before it could be spun, woven, and dyed or bleached in the sun. This cloth was strong and enduring, but thick and bulky compared to the imported calico which later became popular where and when it could be bought, and which fell more gracefully into folds and gathers.

Woollen materials were made from sheep's wool or goats' hair, sheared, sorted, washed, teased, bleached or dyed, spun and woven. Women carried a distaff everywhere, continually spinning the thread, just as they had in medieval times. The cloth was heavy, bulky, hard-wearing and, since the natural oil was left in the wool, rainproof. Thicker cloth was felted, which means it was beaten until the threads were knocked together and the weaving could no longer be seen.

The garments were cut to waste as little cloth as possible. Often the cloth was too thick to seam and had to be joined edge to edge; from this stitching, and from that done to reinforce areas exposed to most wear, such as over the shoulders and round the neck and sleeve edges, embroidery was to develop, carried out with locally dyed threads.

Sheepskin was used for cloaks and coats, and this was cleaned, treated, and decorated, often with embroidery or leather appliqué. Peasants bound their legs, often over knitted socks, with strips of fabric and leather to protect them from spines and rocks. Footwear was simple: in some places, heavy felt boots for winter, shoes made of interwoven strips of bark, and sandals made from pieces of tough cowhide or pigskin drawn up round the feet with leather thongs; the piece left at the toe was made into a point or a blunt upcurved end, and often decorated.

The man wears coat and trousers of natural coloured felt, a white linen tunic with a woven girdle, and a big woollen cloak sewn up so that it could be worn as a hood. Over their white chemises, the women wear "two-apron" skirts, one apron worn at the back and the other at the front. In each case, one apron is pleated. This type of pleating can be seen in folk dress in many parts of Europe; the pleats were fixed by different local methods of dampening and slow drying, and held in place very well.

Although their villages are in nearby districts, the women's costumes show certain differences in cut and decoration of aprons and waist-

Peasants from the Hunedoara region, Transylvania

coats, as do their hairstyles; one woman wears her front hair in many little plaits, the other in twists. The back hair is gathered into a little cap, and a veil called a *marama* was often worn, wound firstly round the head and then the cap, with the ends hanging at the back.

Local differences in dress matter to people with a strong sense of belonging to the village where their families have lived for many generations; each garment was important, not only because of the occasion for which it was made, but also because it represented many hours of work, and would have to last for many years, possibly a lifetime. Bulky and clumsy as it looks, the clothing is adorned with unsurpassed richness: not only are girdles, aprons, and the band on the fringed cloak woven in delicately coloured patterns, but the sheepskin jackets, the tunic front, and the chemises are embroidered with a wealth of intricate stitchery in brilliant colours, chiefly red, and are witness to the skill and creative genius of the women.

When factory-made fabrics became available, and could be afforded, costumes changed: printed cottons and brocades were used for skirts and kerchiefs, and white calico enabled sleeves, petticoats, and some types of trousers to be made very full. From pedlars or at markets, women could buy coloured silks, gold and silver thread, lace, cords, and all kinds of ornamental ribbons and braids with which to decorate their costume.

Peasant jewellery, a study in itself, was handed down from one generation to another. Some items—amulets, charms, and certain beads such as coral and amber—were worn to ward off evil or to bring good fortune; and jewellery in general was a means of showing off the wearer's wealth and status. In many places, young married women actually wore the dowries their fathers had paid for them, in the form of coins, chains, and other jewellery; they also wore, at this period of their lives which was supposed to be the happiest, their most magnificent clothes, brightest colours and richest ornaments.

Most of South-eastern Europe, excluding Russia, came under Turkish domination for varying periods of time, and Turkish influence is strong in many regions. It is seen not only in the use of fine materials, gold thread, coins and dangling ornaments, but in wide sashes, flowing veils, shoes with upturned toes, and the full trousers worn by men in many regions and by women in a few. Two types of Turkish coat, also, have influenced much folk costume, one being the wide sleeveless *giubba* seen on page 6, and the other the jacket with long ornate shoulder flaps; a whole range of Balkan coats are worn with sleeves hanging loose to look like these.

An older influence is Slavic dress. Long ago the Slavs spread from central Russia and settled in parts of Western Europe, from the Baltic coasts to those of the Adriatic and the Black Sea. They intermarried with other races, and fall into three groups: western, southern and eastern Slavs. Their languages have the same roots, and all over this wide area the old Slavic 'white costume' can be found in various forms. For men, it is the white tunic, long trousers, and cloak; for women, the chemise and white head-covering, very like those on page 6, which are embroidered in a very old design. Full, gathered skirts and laced bodices worn over chemises were Renaissance fashion which spread eastward from Italy from the sixteenth century onwards. At the same time, some women took to wearing the Renaissance blouse, gathered at neck and wrists into frills or ruffles. Cuffs and collars were a nineteenth-century addition, and some shirts and chemises are still worn without them.

Later still, in areas nearest to Vienna—the heart of the Austro-Hungarian Empire which, from the eighteenth to the early nineteenth centuries, extended over much adjoining territory—men took to wearing nineteenth-century items of dress, and women put aside their sandals for leather slippers, and their dress became more elegant. In other regions, nineteenth- and twentieth-century dress was not adopted until factory-made clothing swept the old folk costumes out of everyday use. Happily, some survive and can be seen in museums or on folk dancers, and others are still worn for best.

Dancers from Burgenland province, Austria

Gorenska, Slovenia
Yugoslavia

Yugoslavia is a new country. Before the First World War, Serbia in the east and the remote mountainous Montenegro in the west were independent, and the remaining old kingdoms were part of the Austro-Hungarian Empire. Slovenia is the province nearest to Austria, and many Slovenian folk costumes show Austrian influence, right down to the big umbrella.

Both the girls wear full skirts, fitted bodices over Renaissance blouses with full sleeves and lacy ruffles at the neck, printed silk or cotton aprons, fringed shawls, and ornamental girdles hung diagonally from one hip. One girdle is made of silk cord, and the other of gilt plaques linked by silver chains, and both have ornate bows. The headdresses, which are only two of many spectacular Slovene headdresses, are made from large white headkerchiefs folded diagonally and worn with the starched corners crossed behind the head and fastened on top so that they stand up like wings; they are called "white doves", and in the dance, the girls do indeed seem to carry white doves on their heads.

The men wear the breeches, waistcoats, short jackets and felt hats fashionable in the nineteenth and early twentieth centuries, and often seen in European folk costume, to which they have added high leather boots. The colours are dark except for the bright ties and floral patterned waistcoats, and the big silver buttons.

Blata, Bohemia
Czechoslovakia

Bohemia and Moravia are the westernmost provinces of Czechoslovakia, and were for many years part of the Austro-Hungarian
Empire. There was much trade with Central and Western Europe,
and folk costumes were more influenced by western fashion than those
further east, although here and there very old styles of dress have
survived to the present day.

This can be seen in the old man's costume; his dark green coat and
fawn breeches are of fashionable nineteenth-century cut, but his tall
fur cap can be seen in pictures of peasant life as early as the sixteenth
century. Pinned on his lapel are a spray of flowers, and the long pink
ribbon given to him by his bride on their wedding day and worn ever
after for best.

The old woman wears a long-sleeved jacket and full black skirt with
a broad band of brocade and gold braiding; her huge, elaborately

embroidered shawl, with its wide lace edging, is draped over a *coif* (a small cap) embroidered with fine stitching and beadwork. Her white cotton apron is embroidered with flowers and cutwork patterns and edged with cutwork lace. Cutwork patterns are made by very fine stitching round holes cut in the material, which can be filled in with equally fine needlepoint worked in net or cobweb patterns; the material is cut away *after* the embroidery is done, so cutwork is a very exacting skill.

The young woman opposite is just married, and wears the lovely cap and shawl given to brides at midnight on their wedding days, and worn for best during the first year of married life. The pink cap, worn over a lace *coif*, is embroidered in coloured silks with sequins and beads, and her black skirt and low-cut bodice are both decorated with lace and silver braid. Her blouse is in Renaissance style, having full gathered sleeves and a gathered neckline with a "falling ruff" which is only lightly starched so that it falls from the neck in soft pleats.

The little girl is gaily dressed in bright colours and a headband with long streamers of silk ribbon such as were worn by children and young girls. However, in many parts of Czechoslovakia older women also wore colours when the occasion demanded; they had a variety of coloured skirts, each for a different occasion, and worn with the appropriate ribbons, kerchief and apron. Nor did all the women of a village wear the same outfit for a special occasion like a wedding: young women would wear one costume, mothers another, and widows yet another. The same could be true of the menfolk, although their costume was simpler and the differences would be apparent in waistcoats, ties and ribbons. These distinctions used to be rigidly observed.

The young husband here wears a shirt with a small ruff, and a waistcoat, green jacket, and trousers tucked into his boots. His ribbon and posy of flowers are pinned on his lapel, and his top hat is decorated with flowers, feathers and a broad ribbon band with streamers down the back.

Best dress of Blata, Bohemia

Klobouky, near Brno, Moravia
Czechoslovakia

A headkerchief worn with the corners pointing downwards shows that the wearer is going to church; in addition, this peasant woman carries a prayer book and a carefully folded handkerchief, all part of the church-going costume. Her full skirt is worn over many petticoats, and her apron, with brocade streamers hanging in front, is dark blue with a tie-dye pattern known locally as a "bound" pattern. She wears a blouse with a falling ruff, an embroidered bodice and a short black jacket with embroidered cuffs.

The young woman on the facing page is dressed for dancing; the corners of her headkerchief are tied on top of her head, and her ruff is stiffly starched to stand up round her neck. Her high-waisted skirt falls in wide pleats over her petticoats, and her brocade apron has a bow with long streamers at the back, while pink streamers and rosettes decorate the ruffles of her starched sleeves. Sometimes such full sleeves are stuffed with paper. Her little bodice is decorated with a type of Slovakian lace made from many-coloured threads, often including gold and silver. Both women wear high-laced boots.

It is interesting that many Central and Eastern European folk dresses have full high-waisted skirts and falling ruffs. This was probably copied from the old-fashioned formal Court dress worn on special occasions in many of the old kingdoms and principalities into which Europe was once divided. This type of dress, like the many closely pleated petticoats worn in parts of Hungary, also served to make the

Klobouky couple dressed for the dance

wearer look larger; a robust figure used to be much admired amongst peasants.

The young man is also dressed for the dance, and has white trousers tucked into his boots, and a white shirt. His red waistcoat is embroidered in red, black and gold, and he wears an ornate arrangement of ruched ribbons on his shirtfront which, like the rosette pinned on his waistcoat, is the gift of his girl-friend. In some places a boyfriend was given an embroidered handkerchief instead; each boy carried his kerchief, or wore his ribbons, in exactly the same way as all the young men of the village. After marriage, the tokens were put away as a memento of youth, and a man wore only the ribbon given to him by his bride on their wedding day.

Another widespread custom was that a boy could not wear feathers in his hat until he had fought another boy for them, and won them for himself. Then he could call himself a man and go courting. There were many battles over such feathers and plumes, and often the girls snatched them away to prevent them from being torn to pieces in the struggle.

Dancers from Zakopane

The Tatra mountains
Poland – Czechoslovakia

The Gorals are hardy, independent mountain people who live in the high mountain ranges between Poland and Czechoslovakia. Much of this region is remote, and before the last war, the old folk dress was still in everyday use.

The men from Zakopane wear the traditional Slavic trousers, long enough almost to cover the feet, and made from homespun wool, light when new and darkening with age. They are made of a number of carefully cut pieces of heavy cloth, which are joined together with decorative stitching in black; at the front this has been elaborated into an area of bold embroidery and cording in black, enlivened with touches of red and blue. Their belts are very wide, making a kind of leather corselet as well as a means of carrying such necessities as purse, knife, pistol and shepherd's pipe; they are decorated with big brass metal studs, a custom of unknown antiquity which gave added protection to the wearer in battle or against attacks by wolves. The white jacket is worn like a cape, showing off the beautiful embroidery. The felt hat is decorated with bone, or mussel or cowrie shells which were believed to bring good fortune, and in the band is fastened an eagle feather, a sign of poverty.

The woman wears a simple dress: a wide-sleeved chemise with a falling ruff under a bodice and full skirt, and a coloured headkerchief. The bodice lacing is tied in a big bow, and she wears corals, which were very popular among peasants everywhere as they were thought to protect the wearer from disease. Bodice, sleeves, and often the skirt were embroidered in bright colours. Both men and women wear leather sandals drawn up round the feet and laced round the lower leg with leather thongs.

The ferryman from the Dunac river on the Czech side of the Tatra mountains wears a waistcoat richly embroidered in black, red and blue.

Ferryman from the Dunac river

Best dress of the Cracow region

The Cracow region
Poland

Some of the most spectacular Polish costumes were worn among the people in the countryside around the city of Cracow, and in that city itself. At one time, the wearing of Polish costume was a sign of patriotism and not confined to the peasants. One peasant garment in particular was worn in this way, the *sukmana*: this was a loose coat of heavy white woollen material, edged with red and with red tassels at the collar; it is said that the national hero, Tadeusz Koscioki, was wearing a *sukmana* when he swore his oath of fidelity to democratic principles in 1794. The years that followed were ones of trial and trouble, as Poland was wiped from the map of Europe not to emerge as an independent country until after the First World War.

The *sukmana* is worn here over a dark blue waistcoat decorated with red tassels and held together by a wide belt of finely wrought metal; pink and white striped trousers are tucked into leather boots, and the whole costume is topped with a red military-style cap with a peacock feather. The other man wears a similar waistcoat, richly decorated with tassels, embroidery and gold braid, and a belt from which hang three rows of metal discs and red tassels. His black felt hat also sports peacock feathers. The old man wears another type of peasant coat, in dark brown cloth and with a huge pointed collar boldly embroidered in red and gold.

Tinselled and flowered brocades were popular for women's skirts; this one is partly covered by a full apron of cutwork lace and white embroidery. The young woman wears a red bodice embroidered in gold, and with gold tassels; she wears several coral necklaces and, on her feet, the laced boots so often seen in Polish folk costumes.

The tinselled brocades, the many tassels, the gold braiding and the hanging discs are thought to show Turkish influence—the Turks advanced into southern Poland in the seventeenth century—and can be seen in many otherwise very different Eastern European costumes.

The Lowicz district
Poland

The peasants of the Lowicz district possessed a love of colour and ornament which showed itself in all they made, especially their brilliantly coloured homespun cloth. Early in the last century this was chiefly red; then an old-gold dye was made, and this colour predominated. Later, when commercial dyes became available, apple green and lilac were the most widely used, blended and contrasted with other colours to great effect. The woven skirts and short bodices were often decorated with bands of velvet embroidered in silks or beadwork, while the full-sleeved chemises were adorned with delicate embroidery on shoulders and cuffs.

The old couple in our picture wear the red cloth. The peasant woman has a full high-waisted skirt and apron, with another apron worn as a cloak. Her headkerchief is tied in "Turkish" style with a knot in front and long fringed ends behind, and her necklaces are of coral and amber, both thought to ward off disease.

Over his black jacket and striped trousers, the old man wears a white *sukmana* and woven girdle. The *sukmana* was cut in different ways according to district, but was always full or pleated at the back.

Best wear . . .

The young man wears a fitting black jacket with brass buttons, and edged in red; in some parts jackets were waist-length, in others longer and pleated at the back like the *sukmana.* His full breeches are gathered into a waistband and tucked into high boots which, being his best, are carefully wrinkled over the ankles. His black hat is decorated with bands of silver wire and coloured and beaded ribbons. Young boys dressed like their fathers, even to the hat, but very small boys wore petticoats and caps made of sections adorned with beads, ribbons, braids and sequins.

The young woman wears the bright colours and embroidery sported by young wives, also the married woman's tall muslin cap with its goffered frills and wreath of artificial flowers. Women also wore jackets pleated at the back and high-laced boots. Some old people in the Lowicz region may still wear these costumes for best, and younger people for special occasions.

. . . in the Lowicz region

Lithuanian girls dancing the Hat Dance:
l. to r. Aukstaciai, Klaipeda, and Vilnius regions

Lithuania
USSR

Most costumes of Lithuania are basically similar to those of the other Baltic states: the men wore homespun shirts, trousers, waistcoats and coats, and the women wore chemises, skirts, bodices, aprons and, for the most part, circlet headdresses with veils or streamers at the back. While the men's costume varied chiefly in colour and weaving pattern, the women's varied in cut of bodice, pattern on apron and chemise, shape and decoration of headdress, and the use of other types of ornament.

The great variety of colour and woven pattern is seen not only in garments but in girdles, streamers, scarves and handbags. We show you three women's costumes: the nearer girl wears a costume of the Vilnius district (a district can cover a number of villages, each with its own costume). Her fitted bodice is yellow with red and green patterns; her skirt is also yellow with mauve, orange and black patterns, while her apron, veil and chemise are white with geometric patterns in red and blue. Sometimes these patterns were embroidered, sometimes woven, and all showed a high standard of skill and inventiveness. Her circlet is a stiffened band of material woven in yellow, blue and red.

The further girl comes from the Klaipeda district. Her costume is predominately blue, with thin red stripes on her skirt, and red geometric patterns on chemise and apron; her collar and waist-length bodice are edged with white ruffles, and her blue veil is embroidered in white. Her handbag is blue and gold with red patterns.

The third girl, from the Aukstaciai region, wears green with tartan patterns in red, yellow and brown; her pointed bodice, chemise and apron are simply patterned in green and red; her handbag and circlet, with its knot of streamers, match this colour-scheme.

The fiddler on the next page wears green, and his tie, cuffs, knitted socks and woven girdle are patterned in green and red. The other man wears a light-coloured woollen coat, not unlike a *sukmana*.

Here, as everywhere in Eastern Europe, older features of folk costume still survive. Two examples are worn by the old woman: a dark blue coat called "the coat of a hundred pleats", and a white wimple head-dress called a *namitka*. Tradition has it that an invading fourteenth-century Polish king, Jagiello, gave veils of white linen to cover the heads and necks of all women baptized as Christians (the old kingdom of Lithuania was one of the last strongholds of the pagan faith) and that the *namitka* and similar white headdresses date from that time.

Fiddler and old peasant couple from Lithuania

Festival dress from the Tula and Ryazan districts

The Ryazan and Tula districts, Great Russia
USSR

In Great Russia are found types of costume not seen elsewhere in Europe, exhibiting a delight in colour and ornament in spite of the hard life, shaped by the harsh cold winters and very hot summers. The old poverty is gone now, and the people enjoy traditional music, festivities and dancing, and often wear folk costume for these activities.

In districts south of Moscow the women wore homespun skirts and straight tunics, often with long waistcoats, and the girls skirts or *sarafans* (skirts and bodices in one, buttoning down the front); those worn by girls were traditionally black, and those of brides were red. There was a great variety of stiffened headdresses worn over scarves or veils, even in a single district, as you can see on the opposite page.

The woman from Tula district wears such a headdress over a red scarf, and a veil at the back (only girls were permitted to show any hair); it is made of red felt, sewn over a framework, and is embroidered in gold and beadwork. She wears a dark woollen coat with bands of coloured weaving at the hem. The girl from Ryazan district wears a cap with a ruff standing up in front and pompoms of goosedown hanging from it. The older woman wears a fitting *coif* edged with beads or pearls and over it a red headdress with two high points, decorated with embroidery, coloured bands, pompoms and tasselled cords. The woman wearing the sheepskin coat and knitted mitts wears a large warm headkerchief over her headdress.

Most of the clothing is woven in many varied patterns and bright colours, chiefly red; aprons and sleeves are often embroidered as well, and braids adorn tunics and coats and hold the crucifixes. The effect is brilliant and spectacular.

Tunics, the embroidery on which varied from place to place, and loose trousers tucked into boots or *puttees* (strips of cloth wound round the legs for warmth) were common wear for men. The man here wears a dark heavy woollen coat with a woven girdle, and a fur cap with flaps to pull over his ears and forehead. In summer, peasants often went barefoot, here as elsewhere. Leather shoes and boots, and shoes made of interwoven strips of bark were also worn and, during the extreme cold, high boots of thick felt.

a Stiffened felt headdress from Ryazan district
b Woven cap with multi-coloured pompoms from Tula district
c Velvet cap with pearls and silver from Tula district
d Ruffle headdress with pearls and streamers from Tula district

The Arkhangel district, Great Russia
USSR

Some of the Russians who inhabited this northern province became rich by trading in fur, gold, jewels and river pearls; their womenfolk wore *sarafans*, skirts and *shugais* (padded jackets worn to combat the cold) made of heavy flowered brocade in rich colours, and embroidered in gold and silver thread. Chemises and *shugais* had elaborate sleeves decorated with embroidery and pearls; the headdresses were high, variously shaped, and covered with gold and silver, jewels and pearls. Even the poorest peasants favoured brocade when they could afford it, and decorated their best clothes with embroidery, beads and pearls.

The standing lady wears a purple *sarafan* with undersleeves of embroidered and figured silk; her headdress is a halo ornamented with silver, pearls and other jewels, and worn over a little *coif* made of a network of pearls; her red cuffs are decorated with pearls, her buttons surrounded by gold lace, and she wears many necklaces, a jewelled collar, and a jewelled ornament at the end of her long plait of hair. The seated lady wears a *shugai* edged with gold galloons (a narrow braid for decorating garments); her headdress is adorned with gold, jewels and pearls, and strings of pearls hang over her forehead. Another high headdress with a similar fringe (far left) shows the veil which married women wore at the back of the head.

The headdress of the young girl is tied at the back with long ribbons; her chemise is embroidered in red, and her *sarafan* is made of flowered material. The cut of the *sarafan* varied from place to place; those of the north were often of stiff brocade and flared to make the skirts stand out.

The tunics worn by men in the north usually fastened at the side, and the girdles were narrow; trousers were made of patterned woven material, or *naboika* (material hand-printed with wood blocks and vegetable dyes). Summer shoes were made from birch bark and worn with *puttees*, but for most of the year the weather is extremely cold, and felt boots and fur coats and caps, worn with the fur or fleece inside for warmth, were absolutely essential. In the old days, peasants often put a heavy woollen coat over the fur or sheep-skin, and kept their felt boots on day and night!

Peasant costume from Great Russia

31

The Adygei, Kabardino Balk, Caucasus
USSR

One of the autonomous republics of the Soviet Union is Kabardino
Balk in the Caucasus, home of Circassian people, among whom are the
Adygei, known as horsemen and soldiers. Christianized in the sixth
century, they were converted to the Muslim faith in the seventeenth
century; crescents are seen in their embroidery, and women wear the
fez.

   Women's best costume, seen here, consists of an overdress of blue or
crimson velvet, the skirt cut in flared panels, and having long tight
sleeves with long open half-sleeves attached; it is worn over a silk
dress with a frontlet and collar decorated with gold galloons. The

bodice is decorated with gold tassels, and the dress with bold curvilinear designs embroidered with gold thread over padding so that they stand out in low relief. The fez, under a long white veil, is similarly embroidered, and the belt is of chased and jewelled gold with a large buckle; single girls used to wear little jingle-bells on their belts. The woman wears high-heeled embroidered velvet mules, but might wear soft heel-less leather boots instead.

The seated man is wearing a loose high-necked white caftan with a belt, wide trousers, and soft leather boots. The horseman on the opposite page wears, over a high-necked black caftan, a heavy dark felt coat called a *cherkeska* with fairly loose sleeves and on each side of the chest a row of cartridge pockets; the cuffs and edges of the coat are decorated with twisted cords. A narrow leather belt with leather hangings, both ornamented with gold bands, holds his holster and his dagger in a sheath covered with gold and chased in delicate and intricate patterns.

Some readers may think this is "Cossack" costume. Cossack means "a mounted guerrilla" and the Cossacks, wandering bands of escaped serfs, outlaws and adventurers of many races, were renowned as horsemen and fierce fighters. They formed various settlements, and their costumes became very like those of the districts in which they settled. Those in the Caucasus would have dressed similarly to the horsemen there.

White winter coat and hood

Steppe country of Ukraine
USSR

Ukraine is an immense republic, stretching from the Carpathian mountains through the Dniepr basin to the steppes in the east. (Much of central and southern Russia is steppe country: seemingly endless plains, where summers are hot and winters bitterly cold.) The Ukrainian people have a rich tradition of handicrafts that is much in evidence in their folk costumes.

The types of costume illustrated here are found in many parts of Ukraine. The dancing couple wear summer clothes: the man wears a wide-brimmed straw hat, a wide-sleeved embroidered shirt, leather boots, a woven girdle and Ukrainian trousers (this pair is blue, but the colour varied from place to place) so wide that they were once said to be 'as broad as the Black Sea'. The girl wears an embroidered chemise with full short sleeves and a tartan skirt open at the front, the opening being covered by an apron, bright with woven or embroidered patterns that varied according to the district. Tartan was popular, younger women wearing lighter colours and older women darker. As this girl is unmarried, she wears a wreath of flowers with many-coloured streamers at the back.

Married women used to cover their heads with a white veil or a coloured headkerchief, usually worn over stiffened caps as we see here. One old woman is wearing a homespun woollen coat, light in colour and decorated with embroidery or braids; the other wears a fitting waist-coat with flared pleats from the waist. Necklaces and crucifixes were worn, and there was a great variety of woven and embroidered patterns; in general, geometric designs were found in the north and floral ones in the south, the favourite colour being red.

The men wore light coats and, in winter, heavy brown ones with collars that could be used as hoods, like that on page 29. As in other parts of the Soviet Union, in winter everyone wore and still wears big sheepskin coats, fur caps and tall felt boots.

Embroidery motif from a blouse

Woven motif from an apron

Ciangǎi
Romania

This costume shows the marvellous patterned weaving and embroidery for which Romania is justly famous. Here geometric patterns of eastern origin, and those seen in Greece, blend with the floral designs of more westerly regions such as Hungary, to make a peasant art of unique beauty.

The women wear chemises richly embroidered in red, and straight wrap-over skirts with patterned hems and edges, held in place by sashes woven in intricate many-coloured designs and wound several times round the body. Their waistcoats are even more richly decorated with embroidery and braiding. They wear many chains, some with pendant coins, and their heads are covered with long, finely embroidered white muslin *marame*.

The man wears white trousers and tunic, and a dark woollen coat called a *suman*, decorated with bold twining patterns in black braid. He wears a sheepskin cap or felt hat, and sandals made from a piece of cowhide cunningly laced to form a heel flap and a pointed toe.

36

Girl's festal dress with parta

Headdresses of young wives

Rimetea and Colțești, Transylvania
Romania

After the last war, Transylvania was ceded to Romania; but for many years it was part of Hungary, and many Transylvanians are Hungarian, with Hungarian customs and traditions. The villages from which these costumes come are Torockó and Torockózentgyörgy.

*Man wearing best coat,
and couple in summer clothes*

The grandest dress is the festal dress worn by single girls and young married women. The shift is embroidered in red for girls and blue for young wives, and over it is worn a finely pleated white linen skirt, sewn on to the bodice which is fastened with a rectangular embroidered flap called a *fudzo*. The apron is made of coloured silk, and the corded belt with its tassels and gold buckle is like those worn by Turkish nobles more than three hundred years ago; tucked into it is a large patterned silk kerchief. Stockings are knitted in red stripes for girls or brides, and blue for older women, and the knee-high leather boots are black, except for those worn by brides which are red, and carefully wrinkled into fifteen to twenty folds above the ankle.

The glory of the costume is the *párta*—a headdress worn only by single girls, of which there are many varieties in and around Hungary. This *párta* resembles a crown covered in black velvet with three rows of gold lace; hanging from it are many brilliantly coloured ribbon streamers. Young wives used to wear a black silk *coif* ornamented with white embroidery and lace, and hung with streamers like the *párta*. They would also wear a white veil wound around the chin and pinned into folds each side of the forehead.

The young woman on page 39 wears a summer costume of embroidered bodice and apron over a full, wide-sleeved chemise, elaborately smocked above the waist, a corded belt, and a headkerchief. Her companion wears a wide-sleeved shirt and white trousers cut with a flap in front, its edges embroidered, and held up by a black belt; over this, he wears a sash. His sheepskin waistcoat is embroidered in red and has a fox fur collar, and his cap is white sheepskin adorned with a posy of flowers. The second young man wears a felt hat and a dark blue coat decorated with embroidery and red and gold cords.

An embroidered sheepskin waistcoat with a fox fur collar is worn by the young woman in the picture below; it is called a *bunda* and was always worn with the armholes not used, and only by younger women. Older women wore a dark blue or black cloth *mente*, like the one illustrated; it is edged with white sheepskin, and decorated with braiding that simulates buttons on one side and buttonholes on the other, and is probably copied from a cape worn by Turkish nobles. The old man wears a sheepskin jacket decorated with red braid and tassels, and having a fox fur collar; as was the custom, sleeves are empty and hang at the shoulder.

Sleeveless bunda *(left)*, mente *(centre) and embroidered jacket (right)*

The Matyó, Mezőkövesd
Hungary

Hungary has always been a meeting-place of peoples migrating from east and west; among these were the Tartars from south-eastern Russia, some of whom settled in a part of the northern uplands of Hungary and intermarried with the Magyar people there. They came to be called "the sons of Matyó" after Matthias, a great fifteenth-century king who was known as the friend of the poor and whose pet name was Matyó. Because they were poor, the Matyó had to look for seasonal work in other parts of Hungary, and on their travels they saw many styles of dress; in consequence, their own feast-day attire became striking and unusual. Its survival and enrichment is largely due to a famous Matyó folk artist who lived and worked in the district early in this century.

Many Hungarian women's costumes had layers of wide skirts and petticoats designed to make the wearer look stout; Matyó women, on the other hand, wore clothes with long straight lines designed to make them look tall. The young woman illustrated on the next page wears a long skirt with close accordion-pleating which stands out near the hem over a flounced underskirt; her fringed dark blue or black apron

The suba

Matyó couple dressed for best

is long and narrow (only brides wore full aprons) and is embroidered in yellow to imitate the golden spangles once popular but condemned by the Church as extravagant. The long lines of the skirt are accentuated by a tight bodice and a high headdress formed by a kerchief tied over a bun of hair and surmounted by a little straw toque. Over this, the women of one village would wear flower-patterned headkerchiefs with fringes so full that they looked like many-coloured pompoms, while those from another would wear wire-framed headdresses decorated with artificial flowers, lace, beads, plumes and embroidery.

The young woman above also wears a huge floral-patterned shawl, tied at the back to make two long fringed "tails"; the long fringes are thrown out at the shoulder over the full short sleeves of the blouse, which are stiffened with paper inside and have many starched frills above the elbow. Sometimes a full-sleeved blouse is worn, or a warm

42

embroidered jacket which is put on over the shawl; both these have wide basques, so wide that they are folded into pleats standing out at the back. An older type of winter jacket, seen on one of the women holding babies on page 41, is made of sheepskin, and beautifully embroidered on the front, back and sleeves. Black was popular for best wear, showing up the bright patterns and embroidery, and the necklaces of coral and white beads.

The young man opposite wears a shirt with very full and richly embroidered sleeves, a waistcoat with tassels and a fringed and patterned woven tie. He wears a long, fringed and finely embroidered apron over white pleated trousers so full that they look like a wide skirt. His black leather boots are carefully wrinkled into folds at the ankle, and his tall black felt hat is decorated with flowers and feathers.

In winter, men used to wear dark jackets and trousers tucked into their boots, and either the *szür*— the long felt coat with empty sleeves —or the *suba*, the sheepskin cloak worn by the older man; both were ornately embroidered or decorated with appliqué patterns.

Babies also used to be dressed up in embroidered clothes, with a great deal of lace, ribbons and frills; they were carried around on embroidered cushions. Small children dressed in best clothes very like those of their parents; even little boys hardly old enough to walk were photographed wearing tall hats like their fathers'!

Top: full-sleeved blouse and headdress with circular ornament
Below: embroidered jacket worn over a shawl

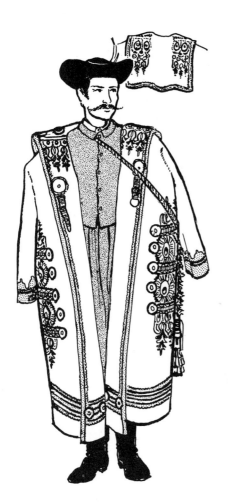

The szür

The Csikós, riders of the Hungarian Plains

When the Turks invaded the Great Plains in the sixteenth and seventeenth centuries, the people left the villages and gathered into peasant townships, leaving vast areas uninhabited except for wandering herdsmen and their horses and cattle. Much of the Plains are still stock-breeding areas, open and uninhabited, the most important being Hortobágy Plain in the west, and the Bugac Plain in the south-east.

The *Csikós* of Hortobágy are matchless riders, and from them the famous Hungarian Cavalry regiments used to recruit their men. They wore, and many still wear, dark blue full-sleeved shirts and very wide trousers called *gatya*; in winter they wear sheepskin or leather trousers. Their leather boots are cut and sewn in the Turkish fashion

44

with one seam on the outside. The felt hat is worn with upturned brim and a feather; and a long whip of plaited leather and decorative leather tabs is carried over the shoulder.

When cheap calico became available and took the place of home-spun linen, the *gatya* and shirt-sleeves, previously loose-fitting, were cut with their present-day characteristic fullness. Those of the Bugac *Csikós* are very full indeed, but this does not appear to hinder their horsemanship.

In winter, when the Plains are snow-covered, the men used to wear the *szür*, a long coat of heavy white woollen frieze worn with the sleeves empty and hanging from the shoulder, with a big square collar that could be used as a hood. They also wore the *suba* (illustrated on page 42), which could be made from any number of sheepskins from three to fifteen, according to the wealth of the wearer; a really grand *suba* would spread out to make a circle. Both *szür* and *suba* were embroidered or decorated with intricate appliqué patterns, mostly in red, the details varying from district to district.

The girl in her best embroidered blouse and apron comes from Kalocsa in the Bugac Plain. Her headdress is made of looped white ribbon, and her skirt, closely pleated at the back and sides, is worn over several petticoats similarly pleated.

Horseman and girl from the Bugac Plain, summer wear

Vrlika, Dalmatia
Yugoslavia

Vrlika lies inland from the long Dalmatian coast, among mountains, and the folk costumes have much in common with those of parts of Montenegro and Serbia, and show strong Turkish influence.

The men wear full-sleeved shirts and dark blue trousers, baggy at the top and fitting below the knee; the younger man has tucked his into frilled white gaiters with red-edged embroidered gaiters over these. Their waistcoats are red, and richly decorated with coins, cowrie shells and, on the right-hand side, a row of interlacing silver rings. Over his sash, the older man wears a belt made of linked silver plaques with red tassels hanging from it, while the younger man wears a very wide studded leather belt. They both wear fezzes with long tassels, and the older man has twisted a striped scarf around his to look like a turban; he carries his wide-sleeved red coat over his shoulder, while the younger man wears a shaggy fur cape. Their pigskin sandals have pointed toes, a type of sandal seen in most of the folk costumes of the Balkan regions.

The women wear full-sleeved chemises, embroidered on the front and sleeves in geometric patterns; one has a hip-length black waistcoat with a bold pattern in red, green and gold braid, and the other a long dark-blue sleeveless coat with red braiding and rosettes. Both wear striped woven sashes, patterned knitted socks, leather shoes with upturned points, and an array of silver chains and coins. Their white veils are arranged in different ways over their scarlet fezzes, one being held in place by upstanding jewelled ornaments. A particularly spectacular feature of the costume, however, is the apron of the younger woman which is made of heavy woollen cloth, fringed, and woven in bold geometric designs of bright colours on a dark background, while that of the elder is made of pleated dark cloth. It is a fine sight to see the brilliant varied patterns of the aprons and the swirl of the wide-skirted chemises when the girls are dancing.

47

The Mirdites
Albania

The Mirdites live in the mountains of northern Albania, and like many other mountain-dwellers, keep themselves to themselves and take pride in their old traditions. There are various groups of Mirdites, some Muslim, and some, like those pictured here, Christian. The women are skilled at embroidery, and come to market to sell embroidered jackets, aprons and saddlebags. The costumes illustrated show the best dress in all its finery, as well as everyday clothes. Women's basic garments are a full-sleeved white chemise worn over long white trousers, sometimes a small open black bodice, a long sleeveless white woollen jacket embroidered in red and gold, a sash, and an unusual little long-fringed red apron. A dark blue headkerchief, chains, coins and a crucifix complete the outfit.

To the festal dress is added a crimson jacket with gold-embroidered cuffs, an extra green-fringed apron over the red one, many more chains and coins, an ornate crucifix, and socks knitted in red, white, green, gold and crimson patterns. These socks widen above the ankle to fit over the white trousers. The headkerchief is gold and red, and worn over a red cap with a row of coins on the forehead. Brightly coloured kerchiefs are sometimes wound round the waist or tucked into the sash, and the girl in her best dress has several of these.

Her partner wears the mountain-dweller's narrow white woollen trousers, strikingly decorated with black braiding and bobbles along and surrounding the joins of the various pieces of heavy cloth from which they are made; the front of his waistcoat is cut in pointed curves and is also decorated with black braid and bobbles. He wears a white fez and, like the girl, stockings knitted in coloured patterns inside his sandals.

These clothes were in everyday use just before the Second World War, and it is likely that they are still worn in the more remote places.

48

*Best dress, and everyday dress
showing the red and gold embroidery
on the back*

Dancer from Samokov,
and couple from the Sofia district

Samokov, Lovech, and the Sofia district
Bulgaria

Many Bulgarian costumes originated in those worn by Slavonic tribes who settled in the Balkans, while others show Greek or Turkish influence. A form of women's dress found chiefly in central Bulgaria is the *sukman*, a blue, black or red overdress, usually without sleeves. This *sukman* from the Sofia district is black, strikingly decorated with white braid and with a hem edging of yellow braid and coloured bobbles; a narrow apron is usually worn, but is omitted here to show the decoration. The white chemise is embroidered in red and black, with lace at wrists and hem. The girl wears a headkerchief and flowers in her hair, a necklace of coins and a belt with big silver clasps. Large clasps and buckles are a feature of many Bulgarian costumes; they are often embossed with a Russian eagle because, under the Turkish occupation, this symbolized the people's hope that the Russians would set them free.

The young man wears long white trousers, and a black or dark blue jacket decorated with tufts of wool and white braid. His shirt is embroidered in many colours and his girdle is woven in dark blue and white. He wears a fur cap, and cowhide sandals.

The girl from the western district of Samokov wears another type of dress, the *saya*: a dark-coloured coat-like overdress, with long or short sleeves, worn with a narrow apron to cover the front opening. *Sayas* are cut low in a curve in front to show the finely embroidered chemise, and the breast, sleeves, and hem are decorated with braids and embroidery. The chemise sleeves are full and embroidered in red, and the belt worn over a sash has a silver buckle.

The old woman from Lovech in the north wears, over her white chemise embroidered at hem, neck and sleeves, a two-apron skirt; the back apron, made of closely pleated woollen cloth, is overlapped by the straight front one woven in a multiplicity of patterns that would vary from place to place. Over this, she wears a long sleeveless waistcoat and a belt with silver buckles. Her headdress is a high *coif* covered with a headkerchief, over which is worn a white veil, and she wears knitted footless socks and leather shoes.

The old man wears dark brown waistcoat and trousers, cut very full, and his legs are bound with *puttees* held in place by leather bands. His sandals are of cowhide, his cap of black sheepskin, and both the girdle and the embroidery on his wide-sleeved shirt are red.

Old peasant couple from Lovech, Bulgaria

Tirana
Albania

The people of northern Albania claim to be the oldest race of Europe, the original inhabitants of that mountainous country before the invasions of other races. They were long under Turkish rule and many Turks settled there; Turkish influence is still seen in their way of life, and in costume. Since the last war there have been great changes, but until that time, many people wore traditional dress, in cities as well as in the countryside.

The city lady wears a full-sleeved white blouse and a brightly embroidered bodice. Her full trousers could be made of as much as ten yards of material; they were cut to allow for many gathers, and an enormous gusset that was fastened into the waistband; at each side, the material was gathered into anklets. It was not unusual for Christian women to wear such trousers. Headkerchiefs were worn and Muslim women, especially the older ones, often wore veils covering the face.

The man wears a crimson jacket with open sleeves, the front cut into pointed curves and covered in heavy gold braiding. This jacket, his full white trousers, white fez, and brightly coloured sash wound several times round his body, all show strong Turkish influence. But over the red jacket he wears a very different garment, a short jacket made of cloth woven from the wool of black sheep, edged with black sheepskin, and decorated with black braid and big black pom-poms on the shoulders. This is called a *Skanderbeg* jacket, after the hero Skanderbeg who waged war against the Turks in the fifteenth century, and who wore such a jacket. Many Albanians wear *Skanderbeg* jackets as a symbol of their struggle for freedom and independence.

The island of Skyros
Greece

The Greek islands all have their own costumes, and some of these are still worn for best. The young woman is wearing a "Golden dress" (see also page 56), remarkable not so much for its goldwork as for the number of its garments, worn one over the other. The custom of almost hiding the bride in her attire could have originated in the eastern tradition of veiling her so completely that she could not be seen; indeed, in many parts of the world brides were hidden from their grooms until the actual wedding and sometimes even after it. On the other hand, the fine garments and jewellery in which brides were arrayed for their weddings formed part of their dowries and denoted their wealth and social standing.

Over a white petticoat she wears an embroidered chemise and an over-chemise of locally woven gauzy material, the upper part red or green, and the lower part white, all skilfully embroidered with the patterns worked in her village. Over this comes a pleated brocade skirt, a bodice edged with white fur, and finally a jacket with wide embroidered sleeves. She wears a woven belt with large metal clasps, and ornately embroidered slippers inside embroidered mules. Her headdress is made of three headkerchiefs: firstly, a plain white cotton one tied at the nape of the neck; then a long silken *bolia* wound round her head and beneath her chin so that the ends, embroidered with patterns of figures, ships and birds, hang down her back; and lastly, a coloured kerchief with a circular pattern worked in gold over her forehead.

The old woman wears a chemise with wide sleeves embroidered at the hem, and over it a fitting bodice cut low in front, and a wide-sleeved black and green coat. Her dark blue skirt is accordion-pleated, with a broad band of coloured material at the hem, and she wears a woven belt with a roundel of gold stitchery. Over a white headkerchief she wears a second one, locally woven in red, blue and white.

Shepherd, with old woman and young married woman in best clothes

The shepherd wears a fine linen shirt with wide embroidered sleeves, very wide blue cotton trousers, a sash, and an embroidered waistcoat. Sandals are worn over his white woollen gaiters with their black garters. The way in which the lace-edged headkerchief is arranged and tied is important as it denotes both his district and the occasion. Shepherds always carried crooks and shoulder-bags; these bags, embroidered or woven in many colours, were an essential part of a shepherd's costume in many regions of Greece and other Balkan countries.

Attica region, near Athens
Greece

Greece has known many wars and occupations, in particular the long rule of the Turks; but many peasant communities have lived and worked in the mountains and isles of Greece since ancient times, and have a strong feeling of belonging to their country and their own villages. For many centuries their dress was very simple; in fact, the Turks at one time forbade them to wear rich clothes or bright colours, so the Christian peasants took pride in simple homespun clothing. After the seventeenth century, there was more interchange between Turk and Christian, and as a result many peasant costumes were enriched with silk, brocade and embroidery, and the wearing of silver ornaments, chains and coins.

In many parts of Greece, the richer peasants wore a magnificent costume for special occasions; this was a bridal dress, called the "Golden dress" because of the heavy gold embroidery with which it was frequently covered. (The Greeks became famous for this goldwork, and made and embroidered regional clothing for countries as far away as Ethiopia.) The "Golden dress" was worn for very best until the birth of a first child, when the rich garments would be passed on to the daughters of the family as part of their wedding attire.

The skirt, bodice and double jacket are embroidered in gold; the bodice is hidden by a frontlet or stomacher made of a network of gold beads and coins, and an ornament consisting of ten rows of little chains and coins. The young woman's hair is plaited into a long plait, at the end of which is an ornament called a *peskoulia* with gold buttons and long tassels.

The young shepherd wears a *fustanella*, descendant of the military tunic of ancient Greece, now rarely worn except by certain regiments. The *fustanella* has two hundred pleats and is called the "Bridegroom's coat" because, if she could afford it, the bride would send one as a wedding gift to her groom. Under this he wears fitting white trousers

The Greek "Golden dress"
with detail of peskoulia

Shepherd wearing fustanella *or "Bridegroom's coat"*

with dark blue or black gaiters and tasselled garters, into which
would be woven his name and the date of his marriage. He wears a
red cap with a long black tassel, and his double-breasted waistcoat is
blue; an older man would wear black.

The woman on the left is wearing the costume a young wife would have put on soon after her marriage as a sign of her new status. She wears a sleeveless cotton chemise embroidered at the hem in a geometric pattern; over this comes a short bodice with half-length embroidered sleeves and wide undersleeves, and then a white woollen garment embroidered in blue called a *sigouni*; the making and embroidering of *sigounis* was the work of highly skilled women. Her apron is made of patterned woven material and, over a red girdle bound six times round her waist, is fastened a wide belt with silver buckles. Her yellow *bolia*, the long veil that is part of most Hellenic costumes, is delicately embroidered, and her jewellery is silver-gilt.

Embroidery motif from a woman's jacket

Vlach shepherdess from Greece, and Albanian Vlach family

The Vlachs
Albania and Greece

The Vlach people originally came from Romania where they gave their name to the province of Wallachia; many still call themselves Rumani, and their language is akin to Romanian. They became herdsmen and traders, travelling all over the Balkans and into Europe. Now only a few groups remain, nomadic herdsmen living in the mountains of Albania and Greece. Every year, they led their sheep and goats from the mountains to the coast in search of pasture, living in tents loaded on to ponies when they travelled, along with babies, chickens, household things, and fleeces and skins of their herds. The women worked very hard: it was not only their task to cook and care for their families, but to pitch and strike camp, and to spin and weave the cloth from which they made clothing for the menfolk and themselves. The material was dyed in various shades of dark blue and grey with interwoven patterns or stripes of black, white and shades of pink. They even found the time to knit, and to embroider their chemises as well as their bodices and best aprons. Before the Second World War, when the photographs were taken from which these pictures are copied, this was how they lived, and it is possible that in the mountains some of the Vlach people are still living in the old way.

The shepherd wears dark trousers, wide at the top and narrowing to tuck into gaiters, a sash wound round his waist, a short dark jacket, and a cap made of sheepskin or heavy cloth; he carries the shoulder-bag used by so many Balkan shepherds, woven in coloured stripes and patterns.

The young shepherdess in the group illustrated on page 59 wears bodice and pleated skirt sewn together, and over this a sleeveless jacket with a fitting top and full pleats at the back, reminiscent of the Turkish *giubba*. Her chemise has wide uncuffed sleeves, and she wears a best apron made from three sections of material joined together and decorated with cording and embroidery. Her leather shoes have pompoms and upturned toes, and as well as her sash worn low over her hips, she has two red leather belts, one with silver clasps. The small boy is dressed like a little girl, except for his big cap which one feels he must have borrowed for the photograph; it was customary in many peasant communities to dress boys like girls for the first few years of their lives. Older Vlach boys often wore tunics and trousers, as shown below.

The older woman wears a long garment over her chemise, open at the front and covered by a full working apron and a wide sash; it has contrasting sleeves as well as undersleeves, and beneath all this she wears a knitted jersey as the children do. Over it she wears a long sleeveless coat, and a decorative collar consisting of a frill of white and blue material gathered at the front of the neck. Both women wear footless knitted socks, and big headkerchiefs wound round their heads over headdresses which have a small point in front. This type of headdress can also be seen on the two little Vlach girls from the Albanian mountains in the final drawing, and the custom of dressing boys to look more like girls will again be noticed.

Key to Map

The numbers before the key items refer to those on the map. The numbers after them are page references. Italic figures refer to illustrations.

Map of Eastern Europe

Index